Fly Tying for Beginners

A Fly Tying Instruction Guide on the Techniques and Patterns to Tie 15 Modern Flies for Catching Fish Plus Tips, Tools and Materials to Get You Started

By

Eden Vargas

Disclaimer

This publication is designed to provide competent and reliable information regarding the subject matter covered. However, the views expressed in this publication are those of the author alone, and should not be taken as expert instruction or professional advice. The reader is responsible for his or her own actions.

The author hereby disclaims any responsibility or liability whatsoever that is incurred from the use or application of the contents of this publication by the purchaser or reader. The purchaser or reader is hereby responsible for his or her own actions.

Table of Contents

Introduction

Fly tying is one of the intricate techniques that support anglers in their fishing adventure. It involves tying thread, wool, and other synthetic materials to create a final outlook that bears a remarkable resemblance to actual flies. So, this way, you can make lures that are suitable for fishing. The skill involves more than just the tying together of fibers, as you might need to learn how to use some tools and wind some materials. There are several inner techniques like the winding on threads, the drawing of gill lines on the flies' bodies, the construction of wings, legs, tails, the lacquering of their bodies, and so many other techniques that you will need to learn; that is why this book, *Fly Tying for Beginners*, was written.

This book contains every detail you need to make most kinds of flies that can trap fishes, beginning from the techniques you will employ, the materials you will use, and the steps you will follow to set up your fly tying workspace. Apart from these, fifteen fly tying beginner projects with visual imagery are discussed to get you started with making your first fly tying project; this will also help you implement what you will learn in each chapter of this book.

With the knowledge encapsulated in the pages of this book, you can be sure to transition from being a beginner fly tying newbie to being a professional in the art.

So, let's begin.

Chapter 1

Essentials of Fly Tying

What is Fly Tying?

Fly tying is a technique that involves making artificial flies with the sole aim of catching a fish. On the other hand, angling is the process of catching a fish with a fishing line and a hook attached to it. This hook in question usually bears bait for the fish, so instead of using baits, the concept of fly-tying comes to play. With the art, you can create flies that bear a great resemblance to real flies that fishes love to see. So, they eventually get lured to them, and consequently, get trapped. The art of fly tying involves the knitting, knotting, tying-in, trimming, and binding of various materials to a hook with the aid of thread strings. If you know the kind of insects your favorite fish love to eat, you can make them and then lure them to the fly you tied. You will need a few tools like a vice, a bobbin, a pair of scissors or pliers, and materials like feathers, hairs, and thread strings for this art. These things will help you in making the right type of fly on your hook.

History of Fly Tying

Fly tying is an art that was birthed from the idea of fly fishing in a time as late as the nineteenth century. Fly fishing is one of the techniques in angling that involves using a lure of light-weight to catch fish. These light-weight lures are known as artificial fish. So, you cast out the fly with the aid of a fly rod and a reel. Over the years, the method of fly-tying has remained the same, with the exclusion of the kind of materials used, which has evolved with time. More synthetic materials that bear a striking resemblance to natural flies have been introduced into the art, and the idea has gone a long way to help in the trapping of fish more easily. Centuries ago, flies were tied without the aid of a hook vice that held them in place. Instead, fingers were used as a platform upon which the flies were tied. Other tools like the hackle pliers and the bodkins have pretty much remained in vogue over the years.

How Does Fly Tying Work?

Fly tying is a relatively simple art that involves utilizing tools like craft knives, bodkin needles, whip finishers, vices, bobbins, hackle pliers, and so on. These tools work on delicate materials like feathers, fur, thread strings, tinsels, and so on. So, when studying this art, there are a few things you have to put into consideration.

- How do you place a hook in a vice?
- How do you wax a tying thread?
- How do you tie a thread string to a hook's shank?

There are many more questions whose answers you need to know to get started, and in this outline, we will be dealing with a lot of them. You might also want to consider other safety tips like those tied to protecting your fingers while you fix a hook to a vice, how not to snap the tying thread on the hook's edges, and how to work properly waxed thread string. Of course, there are more things you will need to know about, but first, let's learn the most important tips!

A hook in the vice

When you fix your hook in the vice, you have to ensure that the hook's mouth is safely tucked within the vice. Also, the hook's shank has to be leveled. You should also fix the curve in such a way that you can see the gape. Anything other than this only spells out danger! If the hook's mouth points out of the vice's grips, you risk having your tying thread snap as you tie. Your skin could even get cut through by the sharp tip of the hook. So, to avoid that, run the pad of your thumb across the side of the vice to be sure that your skin doesn't get caught by some sharp edge. If it does, readjust it. Also, you should never fix the whole gape of a hook in the vice's grips. That will only destroy the hook's temper.

Waxing the tying thread

You can start by gripping one end of the thread with your right hand. The wax will be in your left hand. Now, set the long end of the line above the wax. Work the thumb of your left hand against the thread by pressing it lightly into the wax. Afterward, draw your right hand away from the left until the whole length of the tying thread is waxed. This technique will prevent the thread string from breaking along its size and reduce the case of adhesion.

Now that we know the two preliminary details, let's run through the steps that will guide us to starting with the art of fly-tying.

1. Grip one end of the waxed thread at right angles to the hook's shank. The short end of the thread string should be in your left hand. Ensure that your fingers are close to the hook's shank.

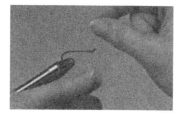

2. Take the longer end of the thread to the far side of the hook, and then go beneath the shank while ensuring that you go back up the near side. You will notice that the longer end traps the shorter end against the hook's shank.

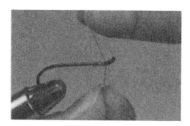

3. Use your right hand to wind three or more tight turns of thread towards the tail end of the hook. As you follow through with this process, ensure that you keep the thread's short end secure.

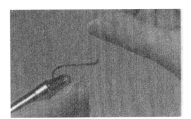

4. Cut off the short end closest to the turns of securing thread. Then, continue winding on tight turns till you get to the point where the tails begin to get tied in.

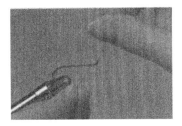

5. The next thing you will do will is determined by the kind of fly pattern you want to tie.

So, we will leave it at this for the time being, as we will delve deeply into the end-end process of tying flies in subsequent chapters. This is just to give you a preliminary idea of how to get started with fly tying.

Benefits of Tying Your Flies

Why would anyone choose to sit behind a desk and craft out nothing but flies?

What are the benefits of tying your own flies?

1. Tying flies is the extra thing you need to finish off your fishing experience. Do you know the immense joy you would feel just by getting to catch a fish with a fly that you created by yourself? It means that the fly looked so natural and beautiful that the fishes couldn't help but be attracted to it.

2. You get to unbox tons of creativity stacked away somewhere in your head! Do you know that you could even create flies that do not even exist in

actual life? You could work with several colors of materials, build your patterns, alter the record shapes, and generally change the style! Making your flies means that you don't have to follow the set down protocols and designs. This way, you even get to think more about the fish you want to catch. What color of the fly would it get attracted to best? What kind of fly does it always get attracted to?

3. You can be assured of the quality of the materials used for tying the fly. You are the one responsible for getting these materials, so why not? You can even add a few qualities that will make your fish stand the test of time, and that's fine.

4. You could even venture into selling the flies to anglers and other fishers and then make a living out of it!

Chapter 2

Fly Tying Terminologies

After shaft: This word is attributed to that of a soft secondary feather. It is the lower part of the feather strips of pheasants and other birds.

Attractor: This term describes a fly that is not usually eaten by fish but has a color and structure that fishes get lured by. This definition plays out best when a person gets creative in the tying of flies.

Badger: This is a kind of plumage with a dark central spot.

Barb: This word defines a section of a hook or each of the tufts of feather fixed to its stalk length.

Barbless: This term plays out best in the catch-and-release type of fishing. It is a kind of hook with no tufts of the feather attached to it—a bare hook.

Barbule: The tiny fibers that line a feather's barb.
Bend: The curved part of the hook.

Beard: This is a definition that describes a situation where the hackle lies beneath the hook only.

Biot: A barb from the short side of a wing quill.

Bobbin: You will use this tool for griping a string of tying thread.

Bobbin threader: This tool will pass the tying thread through the bobbin.

Cement: Also known as the head cement, it is used to finish the windings of thread at the head of the fly.

Collar: The hackle that you wind about the shank of a hook is called the collar.

A dry fly: A kind of fly that can float on water.

Dubbing: A process of winding fur about the length of a piece of tying thread.

Dubbing needle: This tool is used to tug out a dubbing material.

Embossed tinsel: This tinsel can reflect things.

Eye: This word describes another part of a hook.

Fly body hook: A type of hook that has a wire string pointing backward. It is used for making the extended part of a mayfly body.

Gape: This term describes one of the hook's dimensions.

Hackle: This is the feather that you pluck from the neck or the back of a bird.

Hackle Pliers: This tool helps to hold on to the feather.

Hair stacker: This tool will ensure that the tips of the hair tufts are well aligned.

Half hitch: This word describes one of the simplest techniques that can be used to get a thread string knotted.

Herl: This word refers to the short fibers on the stalk of a peacock's feather or the plume of an ostrich.

Keel Hook: This is a type of hook that helps to weed out fibers.

Lacquer: This term describes the head cement that comes in several colors.

Latex: This word defines thin strips of rubber that are either tanned or dyed in different colors.

Marry: This term, in this context, defines the process of winding a wing's quill with other parts in the same curve of the feather.

Mayfly: This fly is one that you will find in an area with fresh water.

Monofilament: This is a single strip of a transparent nylon line that you can use to tie a fly that you will only find in an area with saltwater.

Mylar: This is a flat and colored tape that is used as a tinsel.

Nymph: This is a form of a fly that exists during the metamorphosis stage before it becomes an adult fly.

Quill: This is a word used to describe the feathers from a bird's wing.

Shank: This word describes another part of the hook.

Streamer: This is a kind of fly with the same structure as small fish and is usually a mass of feathers.

Tinsel: This is a ribbon-like strip that is constructed from either plastic or metal.

Underfur: This refers to the fur closest to the skin.

Wet fly: This fly does not float on water.

Chapter 3

Fly Tying Tips and Tricks

1. Get as much information as you need on the concept of bits, fish tying techniques, fish tying materials, and the feeling of being around water. These details will go a long way to furnish your knowledge about fly tying.

2. Ensure that the tips of your tools are kept clean and sharp. Materials like the tail of a buck can decrease the sharpness of your blade rather quickly. So, to cut through this issue, you can sharpen the edges of your tools with a ceramic sharpening stick. You could also choose to get a sharpener for this purpose.

3. You can make your epoxy glue on white and square paper pads. The paper pads can be cut out on a 4 x 6 board with a craft knife. After cutting, you can go ahead to add cement glue to either of the four sides.

4. You can store your thread rolls by getting a small rack for them. This will help you to have your

threading materials within your reach in your tying area.

5. To store materials like feathers, Flashabou, and lead eyes, you can get about 40mm deep cans. This technique will also prevent the materials from being all over your tying area.

6. Get a tool caddy that you can keep your tools in. This idea will help you keep your devices in one place and prevent scenarios where they get lost or damaged.

7. You can crimp the ends of a monofilament weed guard with a pair of pliers with serrated edges. To do this, fix the weed guard's end in the pliers' mouth and then press down on it. This technique will help make several grooves along the weed guard's edges and a flat spot where you can tie your material in.

8. Flatten your hackle's quills before you go ahead to tie them on the side of a streamer fly. After that, you can crimp the quills with a pair of pliers with flat blades. This technique solves the issue of the quill's hackle turning to the side under the thread's torque instead of just lying flat against it.

9. To make microfilament eyes, work with your vice tool. You can start by burning the end of the filament and then leaving it within the jaws of a vice to cool down. When burning the filament's ends, ensure that you do not use lighters with wicks running through them. And that is because they release a lot of soot that will make all of the eyes black.

10. Get used to tying your finishing whip knots with your hands. This technique is faster and can easily be managed compared to when you use a whip finish tool. When making a finishing knot, start from the back to the front.

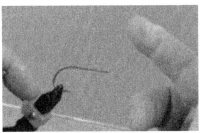

11. To tie a neat fly, wind a threaded bottom at the end of your tying thread that will guide you. Also, as you wrap the thread's tail about a hook's shank, ensure that the line is at an angle of 45 degrees to it. This will make the windings come

out neatly with no form of overlapping or spacing.

12. If you are working with a set of materials you have stored for a long time, you can steam them to make them straight again. Also, if you have flies with rumpled fibers, applying steam to the mass will be one way to set things in order. However, steam must not be used on synthetic materials to prevent them from folding up at the edges!

13. When trimming the ends of deer hair, start by using a razor with double edges. Afterward, suspend the edges over a spray of steam to ensure that every fiber straightens out. This technique will help your next trim to be more precise.

14. You can try threading a feather through the eye of a hook with head cement.

15. Always have magnets in your tying area. For example, if you spill tiny metallic tools like weed gourds on the floor, it will be easier for you to locate them since they are metallic. This way, you can even get to protect your feet from being pricked by the sharp edges of these tools.

16. Arrange your hooks by their names, sizes, and other characteristics peculiar to each of them.

17. Before you tie in any tying material to your projects, ensure that you must have had them checked out for signs of insect invasions. If you find insects weaving through them, you could place the material in a plastic or nylon bag and then have it frozen for a long while.

18. To prevent your eyes from being strained because of lights streaming your tying area, ensure that you use multiple lights.

A Short message from the Author:

Hey, I hope you are enjoying the book? I would love to hear your thoughts!

Many readers do not know how hard reviews are to come by and how much they help an author.

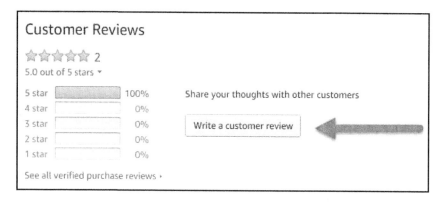

I would be incredibly grateful if you could take just 60 seconds to write a short review on Amazon, even if it is a few sentences!

>> Click here to leave a quick review

Thanks for the time taken to share your thoughts!

Chapter 4

Fly Tying Techniques

Tails In Fly Tying

Several materials can be used to tie flies, and these materials can be used to make the following kinds of tails;

1. Wood ducktails
2. Hackle fiber tails
3. Hackle point tails
4. Fork tails
5. Married slip tails
6. Hair tails
7. Wool and synthetic yarn tails

Now, let's look closely at each one of them and figure out how they are tied.

1. Wood ducktails

This kind of tail can be used to make any fly that has the same shape as the feathers of pheasants, turkeys, swans, or geese.

- Get your wood duck feather marked by tugging off the lighter tufts that line the bottom of the shaft.
- Get the hook ready by winding the tying thread down the hook's shank. Ensure that each turn of the thread is close to the other and that it goes on to the tail level.
- Pick out a wood duck feather that is as broad as the size of the hook you are working with.
- Grasp the feather firmly with your left hand and then pull it away from the stalk.
- Shift the feather to your right hand by grasping the ends.
- To decipher the length of the tail, place the feather above the hook's shank.
- Grasp the feather, and the hook's shank tightly with your thumb and your index finger.
- Hold the tying thread closely to the hook and then push it slightly upwards while ensuring that it is safely hooked to your left thumb and the hook's shank.
- Keep on holding the tail and the hook tightly as you make a loop by passing the tying thread across the bottom and down the other side.

- Tug the tying thread downwards so that the loop makes the first turn.
- With your left hand still in position, make one more loop across the tail.
- Ensure that the looped thread string remains as tight as possible.
- Hold the end of the loop in your left hand, then trim the ends closely.

2. Hackle fiber tails

This tail is one of the commonest tails tied today because you can find the hackles in almost every color. Even if you are making a wet fly or a dry fly, you need not get more than four to six fibers. You get the best hackle fibers from the middle of the feather. When making dry flies, you have to ensure that the threads you use are rigid enough to keep the fly floating. However, if you make wet flies, you can get the threads from any part of the feather.

- Get a large feather from a cock cape.
- With the tip of the feather gripped firmly by your right hand, carefully tug the fibers down as many

times as possible while ensuring that the fibers are at right angles to each other.

- Tug out the soft fibers that lay at the feather's lower half.
- Pick out about six fibers from the bottom of the feather, then use your thumb and index finger to pinch the tips off the feather's stalk.
- Check the length of the tail fibers by aligning them against the hook. Then, tie the tail fibers with the wood duck technique.

3. Hackle point tails

Hackle feathers are too big to be tied as hackles are usually used to make hackle-point tails. Hackle-point tails are easy to make and can stand the test of time. If you need a barred effect for any project, you might need to learn how to make these kinds of tails.

- Get the hook shank ready by winding turns of foundation thread to the tail end.
- Pull out a hackle one-third the length of the cock cape.

- Fix the hackle point to the hook to check its length. Then, pick out fibers that will form the tail at the end of the hackle.
- Hold the fibers you picked out with the index finger and the thumb of your left hand before going ahead to tug downwards and carefully at the rest of the threads. You should ensure that the fibers are at right angles to the feather's stalk.
- Use a pair of straight scissors to cut off the fibers you pulled down. Also, the V-shaped cuts have to meet the bottom of the feather's tips. This place where you cut is defined as the waist of the feather.
- Lay out the feather along the shank near the side while ensuring that the waist and the hackle's outer shiny side face you.
- Hold the hackle point and the hook's curve with your left hand's thumb and index finger while ensuring that the first thread winding moves across the waist. As you tighten this winding, carefully pass the line across the core until the hackle lies horizontally across the hook's head.

- Now, make two more thread windings to secure the turns you made earlier. Then, proceed to cut off the excesses of the hackle stalk.

4. Fork tails

This kind of tail can be used to mimic the natural look of actual flies. For example, to make a fly with three setae, all you need to do is make a forktail with one fiber at one end and two more at the other. Then, when you tie on the bottom in a horizontal plane, place the fibers apart by winding the thread strings several times between them while ensuring that each thread goes under the hook.

- Get the hook shank ready by winding several turns of foundation thread even to the tail position.
- Then, pull out a large feather from a cock cape by tugging at its base.
- While using your right hand to grip the feather, use your left hand's thumb and the index finger to tug the fibers that lie at the lower end of the tail down.
- Cut off the excess fibers of the hackle tail.

- Stroke the left off fibers to their original position.
- Now, use a straight pair of scissors to cut the feather on both sides to get a waist point just below the two uppermost fibers on either side.
- Align the fork tail to the hook shank while ensuring that its waist lies at the rear.
- Tie on the forktail with the hackle-point method that was described above.

5. Married slip tails

This kind of tail is gotten by fusing two different colors of a goose or swan's secondary wing feather. The fusing process depends on tiny hook-like out-growths called barbules present on either side of the feather. They work to hold adjacent fibers present in the same thread, but they can also have a similar thread from a different feather.

- Get your hook shank ready by rolling turns of foundation thread strings to the tail.
- Cut out any of the slips from the outer edge of the swan or goose's secondary feather.
- Cut another slip of the same length as the one you cut above from the same area of another feather's

outer edge of a different color. Ensure that the second feather is from the same side as the first one.

- Place the lower slip on the index finger of your left hand and then the upper slip along with it so that the fibers at the top come in contact with the bottom threads of the upper slip. Ensure that both slips have their dull sides facing you. And if it's their shiny sides that both face you, it's fine too.
- Hold the slip in between the index finger of your left hand and the thumb while using your right hand to join the ends by pushing the back of one slip across the other carefully.
- Hold the joined ends with your right hand and then carefully use the tips of the index finger of your left hand and your thumb to draw out the slips.
- If need be, repeat the fusing technique until you see that the two feather slips are joined across their whole lengths.
- Fix the joined slips to the mouth of the hook, and then check out their lengths. If you see that the two slips have different dimensions, use a

dubbing needle to get rid of the excess fibers from whichever is deeper.

- Tie on the joint with the wood-duck technique.
- Trim off the excesses.
- You are done!

6. Hair tails

All hair tails are prepared in the same pattern. If you are making a fly pattern with short hair tails that require natural and long hair like a buck's tail, you will need to first cut off the skin's full length before trimming the ends to make it easy to be worked upon. This technique will help you avoid having shortened fibers mixed up with the uncut hair on the skin of the buck's tail.

- Get your hook shank ready by winding turns of foundation thread to the tail.
- Use a straight pair of scissors to cut out a full length of hair from the skin or tail, while ensuring that you make the bunch a bit bigger than what you will need for the finished hair tail.
- Hold up the bunch in one hand, and then run your dubbing needle across the lower part of the tail. This technique will help to pull out the more

inferior hairs. Then, use your hand to pull out the rest of the loose fibers.

- Hold the mass of hair tufts by the center with one hand, and then use the other hand to tug out the few of the longest fibers that run across the tail.
- While gripping the longest fibers, tug out the next rows of long fibers while ensuring that their ends are aligned with the first few fibers you picked out.
- Repeat this technique until you have tails of the right lengths. If needed, you could go ahead to realign the ends.
- Fix the tail against the hook to check for its length, but you shouldn't tie on it.
- Hold the tail in its final position while ensuring that you grip it at a point just a few inches away from where you got it tied. Afterward, lift it from the shank.
- Use your dubbing needle to fix glue at either side of the tail, or the front side.
- Fix the bunch at the tail side again before tying it on with about five turns of thread.

- Trim off the excess hair tufts along the shank. Ensure that the overall shape comes out tapered at the ends.

7. Wool and synthetic yarn tails

The number of yarn lengths that you will need to tie this tail on depends hugely on the hook's size and the tail's density. If you discover that one length of yarn is too dense, untwist it and then divide it into two parts with the tip of your dubbing needle. Ensure that you cut out all the yarn lengths at the hackle point for a floss or tinsel body. Then, tie in the tinsel or floss material, and then, the wind turns of thread strings closely about that point.

- Get the hook shank ready by winding several turns of foundation thread even to the tail position.
- Cut off the length of the wool needed for the tail pattern and the hook's size.
- Tie the wool on at the tail, and then continue with the wood-duck tying technique.

- Cut the tail to the length you want to work with while ensuring that you fluff it out with a dubbing needle as needed.
- If you are making a tinsel or floss body, trim the lengths at the hackle position, but then, for other bodies, cut out the sizes of wool so that they drop down the shank.
- Tie-down the excess wool tufts above the shank.

Now, the other styles of the tail for fly tying include;

1. The Golden Pheasant tippet.
2. The Golden Pheasant Crest.
3. The Matched tails
4. The Teal tails
5. The Peacock tails.
6. The Mixed Hackle fiber and ducktails.

Bodies In Fly Tying

Tying in the flies' bodies is the most interesting part of this art and the most strenuous. It is the most important feature and employs different kinds of materials for the best fly patterns. We will begin by discussing one of the most elementary body techniques like dubbing, tinsel application, wool and chenille application, floss bodies, and the methods involved in tying an underbody. We will also study the use of materials like pheasant tails and deer hair, latex, and so many others.

The thorax of flies is another important part of their bodies. For this part, we will study materials like wool, raffia, floss, and polythene. Sometimes, you would find out that the thorax is made of a different material than that used for the body, and that is because they are tied in after the whole body has been completed.

Dubbed bodies: Dubbing, a technique, which you will come across several times in this book, involves the spinning of materials like fur and wool onto a string of tying thread. The dubbed line is then rolled onto the length of a hook's shank to get the rough and hairy look of a fly's body. Now, let's take a look at the basic procedures involved in a dubbing process.

1. Get the hook shank ready by rolling a string of foundation thread to its tail.
2. Use your left hand to ensure that the tying thread is taut and firm enough to hold a good amount of dubbing material.
3. Pick out a few fibers from the dubbing materials you arranged, then place the fibers between the

tying thread and the tip of your right index finger.

4. Fix your thumb on the fibers, and then move it to the right. While doing that, move your index finger to the left to cause the fibers to be twined around the tying thread. Your hands should move in an anticlockwise direction, though.

5. Next, roll the fibers back in the opposite direction—clockwise—using your thumb and your index finger. Continue to move your fingers until you get to the original point you first started in.

6. Repeat the clockwise twining until you see that all the fibers have been wound about the tying thread. Note that some materials like mole fur may not get incorporated easily if you spin them around too firmly.

7. Use your left hand to ensure that the tying thread is taut. As you do that, ensure that you push the first part of the dubbing to the hook's shank. Twisting the dubbing in a clockwise direction will help you slide it up the thread effectively.

8. Apply a second layer of dubbing to the tying thread as was described above.

41

9. Then, slide another layer of dubbing across the thread. Twist it clockwise until it touches the first part.

10. Twist the fibers in a clockwise direction to the point where the two parts touch to join the two lengths to form a single length of dubbing. Here, you can add as much dubbing material as you need.

11. Use the dubbing needle to coat the prepared hook shank with clear lacquer.

12. Now, roll the dubbed tying thread unto the hook's shank. If you need to, trim the excess dubbing material with a pair of scissors.

13. If you want to make a more thickly dubbed body, roll a thread string that hasn't yet been dubbed three or four times until you get to the tail. Then, repeat all the steps described above, right from the first. To get the final body tapered, you could trim the edges with a pair of scissors.

Tinsels and Wires: Here, we will look at the procedures involved in making the body of a fly with tinsels and wire strings.

1. To start, wind a string of foundation thread closely down the hook shank to the tail.
2. For the ribbing process, cut out a length of oval-shaped tinsel, about four inches long. The length depends mostly on the pattern and size of the hook.
3. Fray one ends of the oval tinsel, and then cut off the metallic casing. The frayed part's length should be the same as the length between the tail and the point where either the wings or the feathers will be tied in.
4. Use your left hand to hold the frayed end of the oval tinsel, and then place it beneath the shank and the tying thread.
5. Tie in the oval tinsel by starting just at the beginning of the frayed length. Then, turn the frayed size towards the hook's eye.
6. Cut out flat tinsel, about nine inches long, and if it is wider than 1mm, you can go ahead to trim one of the ends.
7. Grip the flat tinsel in front of the tying thread while ensuring that the trimmed end is closest to the hook's curve.
8. Tie in the tinsel with two turns of thread.

9. Lay the frayed ends of the oval tinsel evenly along the shank.

10. Hold the frayed edges under the shank with your left thumb, and then bind the frayed ends and the ends of the flat tinsel by rolling the tying thread back to the eye. Do this technique closely.

11. Carefully tug the flat tinsel downward while ensuring to twist it in a clockwise direction. This technique will ensure that it comes out neatly at its end.

12. Use a dubbing needle to spread glue layers across the sides of the hook shank, both above and below. Ensure that you apply the layers quickly before it begins to dry.

13. Wind the flat tinsel about the hook's shank evenly while ensuring that the rear end of each turn projects out of the front of the former turn. Ensure that none of the turns climb over the other and that no gap is left. You also shouldn't bother about the excess glue that pops out through the windings. Leave enough opening for the hackle and the wings!

14. Once you get to the hackle, place the flat tinsel in front of the tying thread, and then ensure that the

string is taut. Then, tie in line with three thread turns.

15. Trim the excesses of the flat tinsel string closely to the turns made by the tying line.

16. Buff the flat tinsel upon the body by running across its length a piece of chamois leather. This technique also works to get rid of the excess glue and increase the body's luster.

17. Now, you can wind the oval tinsel around the tying thread while ensuring that it remains taut and firm. Afterward, tie off the line by keeping it trapped with three thread turns.

18. Trim off the excess of the oval tinsel string.

Wool and Chenille: Let's see how these two materials contribute to the body's density by following through with the following procedures.

1. Get the hook shank ready by winding a string of foundation thread to the hook's tail.

2. Chenille of high quality is usually produced in piles. So, grip one end of the chenille between your thumb and forefinger, and then run them down the length. If the texture comes out as

rough, tie in the end at the end of the chenille's length, but then, if it comes out as smooth, tie in the top of the length.

3. Cut out about 150mm of black chenille. Then, prepare about 6mm of it by tugging at one of the chenille fibers. You can leave the cotton strands, though.

4. Hold about 20mm of the chenille strands from the prepared end with your left hand, and then place the strands right in front of the tying thread.

5. Push the chenille thread upwards so that the strands lie beneath the shank.

6. Lock the strands against the farther side of the shank with your left hand's middle finger while ensuring that you keep the long end of the chenille to the left side. Then, you can finish by tying in the strands with two last turns of thread.

7. Continue rolling the tying thread towards the eye by binding the strands beneath the shank with the thumb of your left hand. Then, take these turns far towards the eye to make room for the next windings.

8. Pass the chenille up and over the shank and then continue to wind it so that each turn is in close

contact with the former. The Western Bee has four chenille bands so that you can incorporate the first band for one-quarter of the body's length. You shouldn't see tying thread strings in between the turns.

9. Keep light pressure on the chenille with your left hand, and then use your right hand to untwist the other turns of thread to the point where you are to tie the first band of chenille off.

10. Pass the chenille string to the front of the tying thread before you go on to take the tying thread across the shank. This technique will help to keep the chenille locked.

11. Wind on one more turn of tying thread about the hook's shank.

12. Trim the excess black chenille close to the turns of thread you made above.

13. Tug out the excess chenille fibers from the cut end and the ones left on the hook.

14. Now, you can start to prepare the first band of yellow chenille by tying it in, winding it, and then tying it off. You do it the exact way you did for the black chenille.

15. Cut off the excess yellow chenille close to the securing thread windings before going ahead to tug out any chenille fiber that protrudes from the cut end on the hook.
16. Add bands of yellow and black chenille alternately before tying off the yellow band. Then, you can go ahead to cut off the surplus.
17. To finish this fly body, tie it in a ginger cock hackle, wind it on, and tie it off.

Underbodies: The role of underbodies is to provide foundations on which the final body can be tied upon. If you are tying a big insect, you might need to learn the technique of tying underbodies. They are usually formed from wound-on floss, wool, or any color of propylene yarn, and they occur in several shapes like cylindrical, carrot-shaped, and so on. Everything depends hugely on the kind of fly you are tying.

- Get the hook shank ready by winding a string of foundation thread to the tail.
- Tie in a length of wool, floss, or polypropylene yarn by using the chenille technique. Afterward, wind the tying thread back to the eye.

- Wind on whatever underbody material you plan on working with to any shape you like. If you are working with yarn or floss, ensure that you keep them flat and spread out. Intermittently use your index finger and your thumb to tighten the turns.
- Tie the underbody material off.
- Trim the excess material off and then wind the tying thread in open turns about the underbody back down to the tail. This technique will help to keep the underbody well-shaped.
- You are done!

Floss bodies: The following techniques describe how to tie in, wind on, and tie off floss bodies for a larva pupa.

1. Get the hook shank ready by winding a string of foundation thread down to the foundation's hook.
2. Cut out a floss material of length 100mm.
3. Grip about 20mm of floss at one end with your left hand, and then place the floss right in front of the tying thread.

4. Grip the floss firmly by locking it between the left-hand middle finger and the farther end of the hook shank.
5. Tie in the floss and then continue to wind the thread close to the eye.
6. To avoid a situation where the first wind of floss material moves farther down the bend, lacquer the foundation thread lightly or twist the strands of floss closely to the hook. Then, wind on the first turn.
7. Untwist the floss material and then wind on the tying string close to the eye while ensuring that the floss material doesn't mess with the twists.
8. Tie off the floss at the hackle point before trimming off the excess close to the turns of thread securing the knot.

Woven Floss bodies: First, start by creating an underbody with a smooth surface that has grown narrow towards its ends.

1. Tie in a length of light-colored floss material at the tail, and under the hook's shank, with the chenille tying technique.

2. Tie on a length of dark floss at the tail and on top of the shank, using the same wood-duck tail technique.
3. Pass the tying thread back to the hackle.
4. Grip the light-colored floss material in your right hand towards the farthest end and the dark floss material at a point close to you.
5. Now, start to weave the body by passing the dark floss material over the shank. Ensure that this dark floss material is wound behind the light floss material.
6. Switch hands, and then finish the first stage of weaving. You might need to change hands severally during this project so that the tension applied on the two floss materials is maintained.
7. Pass the dark floss material across the top of the shank.
8. Pass the light floss beneath the shank and then bring it up the near side.
9. Maintain an even tension on either of the floss materials as you weave them towards the eye.
10. Pass the dark floss material over the hook's shank.

11. Pass the light floss material beneath the hook's shank.
12. Continue to repeat the techniques above until you approach the position of the hackle.
13. Keep the same tension on the two lengths of floss as you finish the weaving at the hook's near side.
14. Tie off with three turns of tying thread.
15. Trim the excess floss materials.

Microfilament Nylon bodies: The first type of nylon body used to make the bodies of nymphs was round and finished with matt. You can dye whatever nylon filament you work with to any color that you want. Follow the steps below to learn how to work with the material.

1. Prepare the hook's shank by winding a string of foundation thread to the tail.
2. If you will make a shaped body, tie in a string of floss or yarn underbody. After that, wind the tying thread closely back to the tail.
3. Cut out a strip of nylon—about 4X monofilament is right for an average-sized nymph hook. For a plain body, you will need 230mm of nylon

filament. For a shaped filament, you will need about 500mm of nylon filament.

4. Use a pair of ridged-jaw plier to crimp one end.
5. Tie in the crimped end of the nylon using the chenille technique, then keep the rest length of the nylon clear. Afterward, wind the tying thread in close turns to where the hackle is.
6. Glue the underbody, and then wind the filaments of nylon towards the eye. If the length of nylon filament you cut out earlier is too short, crimp the end of it and tie in another strip of nylon. Now, return the thread back to the hackle position, re-glue it, and then wind on another length of nylon filament.
7. Once you get to the end of the secured tying thread, tie off the nylon with about three thread windings. The excess of this tying thread can then be cut off before you proceed to remove the excess glue from the body with your fingers.
8. To finish the dressing of the nymph, tie in and wind on a brown partridge. Then, cut off the excess of the nylon ends.
9. Finish the fly with a wrap knot before lacquering it.

Copper bodies: Cut into the weave of a scouring pad and then untwist a length of copper strip.

1. Fix one end of the copper strip across the edge of a straight pair of scissors, and then place your thumb on the top.
2. Carefully pull the copper strip through to get rid of any kink along its length. Then, cut off the length that once bore the kinks from the pad.
3. If the technique curls the copper strip too much, flip the strip over and repeat the process more carefully.
4. Prepare the hook's shank by winding a string of foundation thread to the tail.
5. Use black floss to finish the underbody. Then, tie in the copper strip to the body and then wind the thread string over the underbody to the point where the eye starts.
6. Glue the underbody if you want, then wind the copper strips around it with each turn closely touching the former.
7. Tie off the copper strip.

8. Use a straight pair of scissors to trim the excess copper strips. Ensure that you do not cut too close to the area with the blade.

9. Buff the copper with a strip of chamois leather.

10. To prevent the project from getting tarnished, apply a good amount of lacquer to the length of the fly's body.

Mylar and Lurex bodies: Mylar can be gotten in the form of embossed gold or silver foil sheets or in the form of tubes. The sheet form of a Mylar body is one of the most frequently used types. To use it, cut it into a particular length and then prepare it with a tie technique that was discussed for the flat tinsel body. If you are imitating the scales of small fishes, you could work with a weaved Mylar tube. Lurex, on the other hand, comes out in several colors and forms—sheet, flat tinsels, reels, etc.

1. Prepare the hook's shank by turning around a thread of foundation string to the tail.

2. Make a slim yellow or white underbody made with yarn or floss. The color of the underbody you use depends on the color of Mylar you use.

3. Use a pair of straight scissors to cut out a piece of tubing that is slightly longer than the length of the body. This technique is to allow for the material to fray.
4. Hold the tube with your left hand while pushing out the cotton with a tweezing tool.
5. Push the tube over to the hook's eye and then down the length of the shank. As you push the tube down, you will notice that the ends get frayed.
6. Do not trim the frayed ends, though.
7. Pass the tying thread between the near end of the frayed edges. This technique is to prepare for the binding down of the tube's turns.
8. Hold the frayed ends and the hook's bend in your left hand while taking care to wind the turs over the part of the tube where the plaiting starts to fray.
9. Use a wrap knot technique to cover the excess of the cut.
10. Cut off the tying thread and then attach it again to the eye of the hook. Ensure that you do not meddle with the frayed ends much, though.

11. Pull the woven tube toward the bend. This technique will keep on fraying the eye edge of the tube.
12. Keep the tube pulled back, then wound the tying thread down to the hackle.
13. Push the tubing forward, then tie the front end the same way you tied the tail end.
14. Cut the frayed ends close to the securing thread turns.
15. Lacquer the wrap knots at the tail end of the tubing. Then, wait for it to dry before adding a hackle or wing.

Latex bodies: Latex is majorly used for tying nymphs and caddisflies. How can you make a simple latex body?

1. Prepare a hook shank by winding a strip of foundation thread down to the tail.
2. Lay the latex sheet on a flat surface and then use a ruler and a pen with a felt tip to draw a line along the edge. This technique is good for a small hook. For a large hook, draw two parallel lines across the diagonal.

3. Use a pair of scissors to cut out a strip of latex while ensuring that the ends grow narrow. The shape is what determines the kind of tying-in you will work with.

4. Tie in the latex the same way you tie the flat tinsel. Then, take the tying thread into the hackle position. As for the excess latex strip, tie it beneath the hook shank.

5. Wind the latex strip on while ensuring that you apply only a little pressure to the hackle. Also, each turn should cover half of the one before giving off a segmented structure.

6. Do not reduce the tension as you wind the latex strip on. If this happens, you might have to untwist all of the leather strips and then start again. If this issue persists, it's probably because the latex strip is too short. So, to solve it, cut out another strip of leather and then tie it in.

7. Tie in the latex while ensuring that it is still kept under pressure. To secure the ends, wind the tying thread about four-times about it. You can use a half-hitch knot to prevent the ends of the latex strip from loosening.

8. Release the tension on the excess latex strips and then cut close to the securing windings.

Polythene bodies: Colorless polythene materials make more great opaque bodies that are good for making minnows, dace, and other small baitfish. The polythene can be wound onto a prepared shank to make the whole body, or around a part of the shank, just behind the floss thorax. Lastly, you could wind it on top of a floss or tinsel underbody and then have it ribbed.

1. Prepare the hook shank by winding strings of foundation thread to the tail.
2. Cut out a strip that is twice as broad as what you really needed. The polythene should be about 500 gauge and 150mm long. Carefully stretch the polythene strip. This technique slashes the width into two by getting rid of its elastic properties.
3. Tie in one of its ends the same way you tie in that of flat tinsel.
4. Wind the tying thread closely to the point where the hackle should be.
5. For a flat body, wind the polythene in a way that each turn overlaps the other, at least to the point

where the hackle is. Then, take the polythene strip back to the tail end and, again, find your way back to the hackle. You should ensure that you consistently tighten the turns with your thumb and your index finger.

6. For a shaped body, continue to add more layers of polythene before finishing at the hackle.
7. Tie off the polythene with three windings of the tying thread.
8. Cut off the excess polythene fibers.

Pheasant Tail bodies: Use a fine-gauge copper wire to prepare the hook's shank with each turn close to the other, to the side of the tail. For this first stage, using copper wire could be a bit strenuous, so you can choose to use strips of foundation thread first before tying the copper wire strips later on. Then, take the thread to the hook's eye, tie a wrap knot, and then trim the ends.

1. Cut out three copper-colored fibers gotten from the base of a cock-pheasant fiber. Then, tie on the end that is closest to the hook's eye. To make the ribs, tie in a short length of brown tying thread at the tail.

2. Pick out some long fibers from the middle of the pheasant tail feather.
3. Pull the fibers out at an angle of ninety degrees to the stalk before aligning the tips.
4. Cut out three more fibers because you will need more fibers to make a Salmon hook.
5. Use a straight pair of scissors to cut off the weak fibers at the extreme end of the stalk.
6. Hold the fibers near the trimmed ends with the darker side facing you. Then, tie them in using the chenille technique. Wind the copper wire strings in turns close to the hook's eye, thereby locking the excess ends beneath the hook.
7. Build the thorax by winding the wire along the length of the shank. Each time, wind the thread three times to the direction of the eye. The thorax should have a smooth shape.
8. Apply lacquer to the underside of the body, and then wind the pheasant fibers with the darker near the underbody.
9. Lie the pheasant tail fibers after winding them about the body. The first mass of tail fibers might be short of making a large nymph, but then, you can take the wire string across the thorax to the

last turn of pheasant fibers. Then, tie off the ends before cutting off the excess fibers,

10. Tie in another set of pheasant fibers before taking the wire string back to the eye. Then, re-lacquer the rest of the underbody. Wind the rest of the fibers onto the eye before tying them off above the hook with wire. Do not trim off the excess ends.

11. Rib the body with brown ribbing thread strings before tying them off.

12. Wind the copper wire strings over the pheasant fibers all the way back to the thorax.

13. To make a mimic wing case, tug the fibers back over the thorax and then tie the two turns of wire down. Still, ensure that you do not cut off the excess fibers.

14. Take the copper wire strings back to the head while wounding it across wide areas.

15. Take the fibers back to the eye. Then, tie the fibers down with a wrap knot. Ensure that you do not get the fibers kinked.

16. Cut off the excess fibers cleanly while ensuring that you do not block the eye.

17. You are done!

Hackles In Fly Tying

Dry-fly hackles

Simple dry-fly hackles

1. Make the body and then tie it off with the tying string at the hackle position. Afterward, trim the excess material off. Then, trim the excess ends off.
2. Pick out a cock hackle of the right size for the hook.
3. Get the hook ready by cutting a waist portion above the fluffy fibers at the end of the hackle.
4. Cut off the lower part of the hackle that you don't need and then ensure that you leave a small portion of fibers just below the waist level. The triangle will help to keep the hackle in place once you tie it in.
5. Spread the prepared hackle along the near side of the hook's shank with the outer edges facing you and the waist in line with the tying thread. The prepared hackle must not exceed the hook's eye.

6. Hold the hackle with the thumb and the index finger of your left hand. Afterward, tie it in with two thread turns.
7. Wind the tying thread close to the eye.
8. Hold the tip of the hackle with a pair of hackle pliers, then place a nail at the base of the hackle. After that, bring the hackle up to a vertical position while ensuring to twist the ends so that the outer surface is the one close to the hook's eye.
9. Keep your left index finger in place as you wind the hackle over the shank. Afterward, you can go ahead to remove it.
10. Wind on the hackle in close turns while ensuring that the turns do not lap each other. As you do this process, work towards the hook's eye. The hackle should be twisted at the top, and that twist must be maintained during the wind on. This technique keeps the hackle's stalk at right angles to the hook.
11. Before you get to the eye, tie off the hackle at the tip by bringing it to the front of the tying thread. Then, lock it in with two turns of thread across the hook's shank.

12. Cut off the excess tips of the hackle.

13. To finish the fly in a way that you don't end up tying in the hackle fibers, first form a wrap knot. Ensure that you pull all the hackle fibers back with the thumb and the first two fingers of your left hand while you hold the tying thread.

14. Finish the wrap knot by releasing the hackle fibers in a way that the dubbing needle is right at the loop. Then, tighten the loop while taking care not to lock in any of the fibers. If the fibers are locked in, you can cut them off with the tying thread.

15. Lacquer the fly's head with a dubbing needle to clear the hook's eye while it is still wet.

How to wind one hackle through another for dry flies

Winding one hackle through another will help the fly become even more buoyant in water. Follow the techniques below to follow through with the process.

1. From one of the capes, pick out the hackle and a hook that fits its size. From the second cape, find another hackle of the same size and the same width as the first one. The second hackle does not

necessarily need to come from the same quarter as the first.

2. Get the two hackles ready before tying in the first hackle with one or two turns of tying thread. Then, tie in the second hackle in a direction adjacent to the first, with each winding close to the former.

3. If you want one of the two colors to dominate, tie in that color first. This technique is used because it is the first one that will be tied to the second one. If you are making a bushy fly with many hackles, you must tie the body further down the shank than you normally would allow, making room for additional hackles.

4. First, start by winding the first hackle on the first one to be tied in while ensuring to leave spaces between each of the turns. Then, tie off the first wound-in hackle.

5. Wind on the second hackle by twisting it through the first hackle. Do this technique this way to avoid getting too many fibers locked in.

6. Tie off the second hackle fiber with about two turns of tying thread. Thereafter, cut off the ends of the hackle with the edge of the scissors close to

the turns. If you do not cut the excess close enough to the turns, you risk getting big stubs that could block the eye. And take note that errors cannot be hidden with a wrap knot.

7. Use a dubbing needle to push out the fibers, and then finish the fly with a wrap knot.
8. Lacquer the head and then clear the eye before the lacquer dries.

Fore-aft hackles

The name fore-aft hackles are so-called because they belong to hackled flies that have hackles tied to either end of their body. And that technique helps them to float well in water. The fore hackle is usually tied in as a simple dry-fly hackle. The aft hackle is small and, depending on the pattern, can be of a different color. Now, let's see how a Fore-aft hackle is tied.

1. Get the hook's shank ready by winding around its span a string of foundation thread.
2. Get the cockle hackle ready the same way you would a simple dry-fly hackle.
3. Align the hackle along the near side of the hook's shank with the outer edge facing you and with

67

the waist aligned with the tying thread at the tail end.

4. Tie in the hackle with about three turns of tying thread, then wind the thread to the point of the hackle.
5. Wind on the hackle like you would do with a simple dry-fly hackle, with each turn in contact with the former.
6. Loosen the tying thread until you get to the point where you can tie the hackle off.
7. Tie off the aft hackle with two turns of tying thread. Trim the ends of the hackle closely to the securing turns.
8. Tie in the body material with the tying thread at the hackle point. Wind on and tie off the body material before cutting off the excess ends.
9. Tie in another hackle at the fore hackle position. Wind the hackle on like you would do a simple dry-fly hackle. Then, tie it off at eye level.
10. Trim the excess ends to finish the fly.

Dry fly body hackles

Before we head over to the techniques involved in making the hackles of a dry fly, we will consider the Palmer technique. Palmer is the process of winding a cock hackle down the length of the body of a fly, from the head to the tail. Most flies are only palmed lightly with a single hackle technique. If you are going to make a densely hackled fly, you could choose to wind on two body hackles simultaneously or add a simple dry-fly hackle to the head.

Now, let's see how we can make a dry fly body hackle.

1. Form the fly's body, but then, take care not to rib the fly. Then, cut off the excess material. For tinsel bodies, you can hold a palmed hackle in place by tying in the ribbing to the tinsel.
2. Pick out a cock hackle with fibers that run through a length about two times the depth of the hook's gape. Then, prepare the end for a simple dry-fly hackle technique.
3. To make a winged dry fly, tie in the hackle like a simple dry fly hackle behind the wings while ensuring that you leave enough space for the head hackle. To make a lightly palmed fly, tie in the hackle at the head and then wind on about

two close turns of hackle. Afterward, you can wind the hackle down to the tail.

4. Tie the hackle off with the ribbing material.
5. Rib the body toward the direction of the head while twisting the ribbing material from one side to the other side. This technique will prevent the fibers from getting kinked.
6. Tie off the ribbing material, and then trim the excess ribbing as well as the ends of the hackle fibers.
7. Finish the fly with a wrap knot.
8. Use the dubbing needle to draw out any trapped fibers.

Wet fly hackles

Simple wet-fly hackles

The hackles of a simple wet fly are formed from soft feathers and are tied in such a way that the fly gets immersed below the water's surface at once. You can work with hen hackles, soft cock hackles, the feathers from the back, breast, and neck, etc.

1. Get the hook shank ready to form the body before cutting off the excess fibers.
2. Select the hackle of a hen and then tug down the fibers so that they are at angles of ninety degrees to the hackle's stalk.
3. The fibers of the right hackle should just extend beyond the hook's curve.
4. To get the hook ready for tying in, hold the tip with the edge of a small pair of hackle pliers.
5. Use your left hand to tug the fibers down to the point that is just below the tips of the hackle. Now, you can go ahead to release the hackle pliers.
6. Use a straight pair of scissors to cut off the majority of the hackle tips.
7. Continue to hold back the fibers before tying in the hackle tips at the hackle point. As you follow through with this technique, you have to ensure that the outer surface of the feather faces you.
8. Wind the tying thread further down the hook's shank towards the direction of the eye. Then, bind the tip of the hackle. Ensure that the tip does not block the hook's eye.

9. Hold the ends of the hackle with a pair of hackle pliers, and then push the hackle up vertically with its outer edge facing the eye of the hook.

10. Before you begin to wind the hackle on, double it by tugging the fibers to the left. Then, go on to wind on the hackle closely to the hook's eye.

11. Tie off the hackle with two turns of tying thread while ensuring that you leave out the soft part at the feather's base.

12. Trim off the excesses of the hackle's tips, and then finish off the fly.

False Hackles

A false hackle is a mass of cockerel fibers that are tied in and spread evenly across the hook's shank at the point of the hackle. Now, let's see the processes involved in tying in a false hackle.

1. Form the body and then proceed to tie off the body material at the hackle point.

2. Pluck out one of the longest hackles from a cape. A cock's cape will be the most preferable for this process.

3. Cut off the excesses of the hackle's fluffy ends.

4. Tug out a bunch of hackle fibers while ensuring that the tips fall into alignment.

5. Place the bunch of hackle fibers beneath the hook's shank, right at the position of the hackle. Then, shift the bunch to add to the length. While holding the bunch with your left hand, tie the fibers in with about three turns of thread over the shank. Then, wind the turns of thread to the point that is just behind the point the bunch is tied in. This technique will keep the fibers face down. Cut off the excess fibers, then wind a few more turns over the trimmed fibers before tying on a wing.

6. Lay the bunch of hackle fibers at the farther side of the hook, and then adjust the length of the false hackles according to the tied fly pattern. Ensure that the tips of the false hackle are in alignment with the hook's edge.

7. Use the thumb and the index finger of your left hand to hold the mass of fibers down. Then, wind the first turn of thread about the hook's shank.

8. Guide the hackle fibers down the length of the shank carefully as you wind the first turn of thread across it. You should finish this technique

when you get to the hackle point. You should be careful, though, as it can get very easy to get close to the hook's eye.

9. In the final false hackle, the fibers should automatically spread out. The fatter the body of the thorax, the larger the angle at which the fibers spread.

Wings In Fly Tying

Dry-fly wings

Upright hackle point wings

This kind of wing is used for flies that have mottled wings. You would also enjoy using them for flies that bear split wings. Now, let's run through the basic processes involved in tying an upright hackle point wing.

1. Wind a string of foundation thread to the middle of the hook's shank. Then, take the thread back the middle length towards the wing's site.

2. Pick out two medium-sized cock hackles, and then place one hackle on top of the other. After

74

that, align the tips and then check their dimensions. This kind of wing should be shorter than the hook's shank.

3. Get the hackles ready by trimming off the edges of the excess fibers.
4. Place the outer edges of the wings on top of the hook's shank at the position of the wing.
5. Tie on the wings using the wood-duck method.
6. To get the wings back up, tug the wings upwards and a little bit to the back with your left hand.
7. Afterward, wind about two turns of thread in front of the wings, in a manner that they are tied firmly to the base.
8. To split the wings, carefully tug the wing near you in your direction. Then, pass the tying thread between the wings and over the hook's shank. Now, you can let go of the rear wing.
9. Continue to wind the thread beneath the hook's shank and up the near side of the hook, at a point behind the rear wing.
10. Carefully hold the wing that's far from you and then wind the tying thread between the two wings in a diagonal direction.
11. Trim the excess hackle stalks.

12. Stroke the wings so that they go right up.

13. Finish the fly by winding the tying thread across the wings. Do not wind the tying thread between the wings.

Fan Wings

1. The wind turns of foundation string half the length of the shank before going ahead to take the strings back to the point where the wing is to be fixed.

2. Pick out two similar feathers of a duck's breast ad then pull out the fluffy tufts at the base.

3. Put one feather over another and ensure that their tips fall in line. You can further check their dimensions by holding them against the hook's shank. Cut off the excess fibers at the base with a pair of straight scissors before going ahead to cut a waist.

4. Fix the wings over the hook's shank so that they tend towards the hook's eye. Ensure that the waists you cut out are well-aligned with the tying thread. Then, you can go ahead to tie on the

wings by employing the wood-duck tail method. Go by using two turns of thread.

5. Grip the feather's stalk with the thumb and the index finger of one hand, and then tug the stalks downwards with the far wing stalk fixed to the far side and the near wing stalk fixed to the near side. Repeat this process until the wings are well aligned and upright.

6. Free the far wing's stalk, and then hold the two wings between the index finger and the thumb of your left hand. This technique will help to keep them upright.

7. Free the near wing stalk, and then use your right hand to pass the tying thread behind the wings. Thereafter, you can go on to wind about three more turns of thread in front of the wings while ensuring that you lock in the fibers beneath the hook's shank.

8. Trim the excess stalks.

9. The dressing may at this point have the wings twisting either to the right or to the left, or end up not meeting at the base, so you can correct those errors by winding a few horizontal turns of thread around the bottom of the wings. If the

wings twist to the left side, twist them in a clockwise direction, and if they twist to the right, twist them in an anticlockwise direction.

10. Finish the fly by following any technique the pattern requires.

Wet-fly wings

Streamer wings

1. Wind a string of foundation thread to the tail of a hook's shank. To form the body, allow for more space for the hair wing than you would for the hackled wing.

2. Pick out the materials you will use for a streamer wing, and then check out their dimensions. The wing used here should be about one or two times longer than the length of the hook's shank.

3. Prepare the two hackles that will form the inner wing by tying in the inner wing with the wood-duck technique. Cut off the excess fibers and then wind on two more turns of thread to secure the ties.

4. Prepare the hackles for the outer wings and ensure that their lengths run into about half the inner wing length.
5. Set one hackle along the farther side of the inner wing, and then tie it in.
6. Set the other hackle along the near side while following the same technique before going ahead to adjust the length of the far hackle. Then, you can finish by tying it in.
7. Trim off the excess hackle stalks of the outer wing.
8. Then, finish off the streamer fly.

Chapter 5

Getting Started with Fly Tying

Tools And Materials

Tools

Fly Tying Vice

- It has components like a hook jaw and a clamp.
- The hook of a vice has to be held in a way that it doesn't get damaged.
- The best vice to get is a rotary vice.

Bobbin

- This tool helps to secure the tying thread.
- They bear the spools of the tying thread and then pass it down a tube where you can neatly wind the thread about a hook.
- They have parts that alter the tension on a string of threads.

Fly Tying Scissors

- It is used for cutting tying materials like fur, thread strings, lead eyes, and so on.
- You need them to be short with sharp edges.

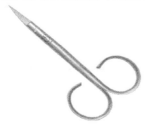

Hair Stacker

- This tool helps to set the tips of materials into a straight line.

Hackle Pliers

- This tool helps to hold the fly, tying feather strips.
- With this tool, there's less wastage of materials.
- They help prevent the hackle fibers from loosening as you tie them down with thread strings.

Hackle Gauge

- This tool helps to measure the dimensions of the length of feather barbs.

- You can work with this tool by winding the feather strip around its pin and then have the length of the barbs measured to scale.

Craft Knife

- This tool is what you need to cut fly tying materials like the foam sheets you use for tying beetles.

Bodkin Needles

- This tool is that long poky thing you need to tie flies.
- It is used to apply head cement and to tug out tiny strips of fur from the body of a fly.

- You can also use it to wipe off excess glue from the eyes of your hook.

Half Hitch Tool

- This is a knotting tool used for tying flies.
- You can use this tool to tie thread strings at a fly's head.
- It is a tube with a small diameter that is used to reach out to the hook's eye.
- You can also use it to tie half hitches.
- This tool comes in several diameters.

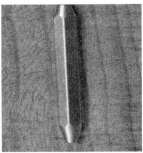

Whip Finisher

- This tool is used to fix a fly tying knot.
- It helps you to tie off your thread strings in the middle of the fly.
- This tool makes better knots than the ones a half hitch tool will make.

Needle Nose Pliers

- You should use this tool to bend the barbs of feather strips.
- You can also use this tool to make a feather strip free from barbs.

Materials

Thread

- They come in several colors and sizes, but you should ensure that you have them in black, brown, and a light tan color.
- The 6/0 size is what you need for tying all flies except for nymphs.
- The 8/0 size will help you tie small and dry flies.
- The 3/0 size will help you to spin and stack deer hair. This one is usually thick and strong.

Flosses

- This material is made from silk.
- It is commonly found in the red color.
- It makes the body of a fly smooth and shiny.
- This material will not help a fly float, so it is often utilized in the crafting of streamers and nymphs.
- It is that shiny thing you will see behind a hook's eye.

Head Cement

- This material helps to secure the tying thread to the head of a fly.
- The common types available include the solvent form that is very similar to nail polish, the UV cure, and 2-part epoxy.

Wax

- This material is usually applied along the length of a wire string to aid the process of dubbing.
- It helps other materials to get attached easily to the thread.
- All you need from this material is a little of it.

Lead Wire

- This tool helps to sink a fly once you tie it to the shank of a hook.
- It comes in different sizes.
- The .020 wire strip is fine enough to be used for making small flies.

Marking Pens

- This tool helps to mark out the gill lines on your fly.
- They will also help you to apply a shadow from the top of a fly to the bottom.
- You can get them in colors like red, black, and brown.

Fine Wire

- This material helps to emphasize the colors you use for a fly.
- They add weight to the body of a nymph or streamer.
- They can be used to segment the thorax of a fly.

- They are readily available in gold and copper.
- It makes the tying of flies relatively easy.

Feathers

- There are six different types of feathers that you can use to tie a fly.
- There's the hackle that is usually winded about a hook's shank to create the wings and legs of a fly. You get the best hackles from domestic fowls. There are two types of hackles; the saddle hackle and the neck hackle. The former is found in a domestic fowl's rump and can be used to make dry nymphs and streamer flies. The latter comes from the neck of a chicken, and you will discover that the finest have barbs with regular lengths.
- There's the marabou that is used for embellishing hats. They are used for tying the wings and tails of flies.

- The Pheasant tail is used to tie the bodies, wing cases, and tails of flies.
- The Primary feather is used to tie the wings of flies. You can get them from ducks. Another name for this feather is called a quill.
- Herls are long strips of feathers that branch from the major stem of a feather strip. The Peacock herl is the commonest type and can be used to tie in the body of dry flies and nymphs.

Hair or Fur

- This material is gotten from the tails of cows.
- They are used for tying the tails, wings, and beards of streamers.

Synthetics

- This material includes rubber for the legs of a fly, chunks of foam for the bodies, strings for the ribs of a fly, and so on.
- They help to add flashing effects to flies, as well as help them float.

Chenille and Yarn

- This material is usually mixed with bright materials and is mostly used for building up the bodies of nymphs and streamers.
- This material comes in the form of strips and can be used to give a fly a fuzzy outlook.

Tinsel and Other Shiny Add-Ons

- The other add-ons discussed here include the Flashabou, the Krystal Flash, and some other plastic films attached to the tails of flies.
- They are also tied into the bodies of streamers to add more flash to it.

Hooks

- There are different types of hooks, each one for dry flies, nymphs, and streamers.
- For dry flies, you can work with a hook whose size ranges between size ten and size 18.

- For nymphs, use hooks with sizes that range between size 12 and size 16. Size 14 is the commonest one, though.
- For streamers, use hooks whose sizes range from size 4 to size 10. Size 6 is the commonest.

Setting Up Your Fly Tying Workshop

The first thing you need to do when setting up a works space is to consider that most of your tying materials will inevitably find their way to the ground. So, you might want to ensure that the floors are covered with thick carpets that will prevent the materials from sinking into holes and grooves. This way, a vacuum cleaner or a block of magnets (if the material is metallic) can easily pick it up for you. Now, let's look at a few other pieces of equipment you will need in your workshop.

The tying bench

- Ensure that the surface is smooth, regular, and free from dents.
- It should also be big enough for you to arrange your tools and materials comfortably.

93

- Get a bench that doesn't wobble while its stands. The four legs must be well balanced on the ground.
- Protect the surface of your work table with a strip of plastic to protect it from lacquer spills.
- Make sure that your vice clamp tool will fit through the density of any benchtop you work with.

The Chairs and the tying positions

- Get a chair that will prevent you from turning your neck around a long bend just to see your vice work.
- You should sit in a relaxed and upright pose.
- Get a seat that can rotate about an axis and one that has a backrest that can easily be altered. Another thing that should be alterable is the height of the seat above the ground.
- Get a seat with armrests that will support your elbows as you tie your flies.

Lighting

- Work in a space with good lighting.
- A room brightened by a fluorescent bulb is just what you need.

- If the above option is not enough, you could try getting an overhead LED light that will focus solely on your flies as you tie them.
- Avoid working in a room that is too bright! That can cause as much damage to your eyes as the one a dull room would cause. So, work with lighting that isn't too harsh on your eyes.

Setting out your workspace

1. Ensure that the vice is positioned halfway along the side of the bench.
2. The vice should point towards the right if you are right-handed and vice versa.
3. Adjust the vice so that the jaws are at a height that is comfortable for you.
4. Arrange all the tools and materials you need on the surface of your workbench by following any pattern of your choice. Just ensure that you place them in points that won't need you searching for them again.

Chapter 6

Fly Tying Patterns

Daddy Long Legs **(Dry Fly)**

Tools and Materials

- Hook: 10 or 12 long shank.
- Thread: Black or brown
- Wings: Two red or grizzly cock hackle points.
- Ribbing: Fine gold wire.
- Body: Fawn raffia
- Thorax: Brown ostrich herl.
- Hackle: Red or grizzly cock hackle.
- Legs: Six fibers from a cock pheasant's center feather tail.

Procedures

1. Prepare the hook's shank with a foundation thread, and then knot the wings made with two blue dun cock hackles to get the body. Split the winds into two parts, and then make inner knots.

Ensure that you are not winding in the knots as you progress.

2. For the legs of this fly, pull off six fibers from a cock pheasant center tail feather. Ensure that these fibers are long enough.

3. Hold up the end of one fiber with your left hand, and then create a loop by rounding the tip about that end.

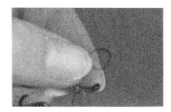

4. Pass the tip of the fiber through the loop you formed in the step above with a fine crochet hook or a dubbing needle. Then, create the first two overhand knots to get leg-joints. You could also go-ahead to use the needle to fix the loop at a point on the fiber. Ensure that you do the loop repositioning before you pull the knot tightly. For a neat angle at the leg-joint, ensure that you don't tighten the knot too much.

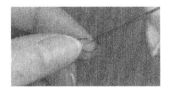

5. Create another knot using the same technique above while ensuring that it is far along the length of the fiber. This step will give you the second leg-joint.

6. Work with the first leg of fiber as a guide for the rest of the five while ensuring that the location of each knot is as close to the other as possible.

7. The picture below is a representation of the six prepared pheasant fiber legs.

8. Tie each leg beneath the hook shank one by one, with four legs behind the wings and two in front. Then, position the legs towards the hook point, just as it is illustrated in the diagram below. Ensure that you secure the thread to be tied each time and that you also trim the edges before going ahead to tie in the next leg. When you are

done tying in all six legs, wound the tying thread to the hook's eye.

9. Pass one total winding of thread behind all six legs. Then, carefully squeeze in the hackle between the legs to divide them evenly. You can start by putting a distance between the first leg tied and the one adjacent to it.

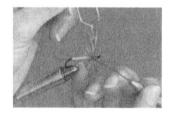

10. Tie off the hackle at the head of the fly.
11. Trim off the excess hackle, and then finish the fly.

The Keel Fly (Wet or Dry Fly)

Tools and Materials

- Hook: 12 or 14 keel hooks
- Thread: tan or light yellow.
- Wings: Cream grizzly cock hackle points.
- Tail: Ginger cock hackle fibers.
- Ribbing: Brown tying thread.
- Body: A bunch of tannish gray deer tail fibers.
- Hackles: Two ginger cock hackles.

Procedures

1. Fix the Keel hook in the vice as illustrated below.

2. Pass a small part of a foundation piece of thread halfway down the curved part of the hook. Then, pass it in wider turns halfway back. Tie two creamy-grizzly upright hackle wings.
3. Fasten the thread to be tied with a wrap knot or a half-hitch knot.
4. Remove the half-heel knot from the vice, and then fix it just as it is illustrated below. To get the tail inclined to an angle of about 30^0, pass the turns of

thread closely down the shank and halfway around the bend.

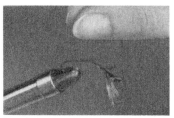

5. Tie on a small mass of rigid ginger cock hackle fibers to form a tail at that 30^0 angle inclination. Trim the excesses and then wind the thread to the position of a hackle. That position is half the curved portion of the shank.

6. Set along with a mass of tan-colored deer hair, and then grip the ends as it is shown below. This way, the ends of the deer hair can form an extra part of the tail.

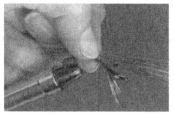

7. Tie the deer hair at the position of the hackle, with three or four close turns of tying thread.

101

8. Wound turns of the thread down to the tail while ensuring to surround the whole shank with deer hair.

9. Fasten the tips of the deer hair at the tail with three close turns of thread. Then, return the thread to the hackle setting.

10. Trim the excess deer hair and then hold down the ends left off while ensuring that you return the thread to hackle position.

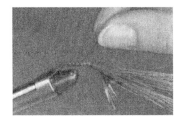

11. Tie in two ginger cock hackles while ensuring that they both have a size larger than that for a normal hook. Then, wound the thread to the eye of the hook.

12. To get the desired two-plane hackle to look, you can start by winding each hackle about the curved part of the shank. Then, you can finish at the hook's eye.

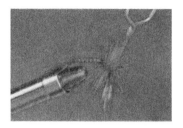

13. Tie off the hackles, and then finish the fly.

Yorkshire Fly Body Hooks (Dry Fly)

Tools and Materials

- Hook: Dayfly Yorkshire fly body hook
- Thread: Brown or black.
- Wings: Starling Wing Quills.
- Tail: Three fibers from a natural bright-red cock hackle.
- Body: Well-marked stripped peacock quill

103

- Hackle: Natural bright-red cock hackle.

Procedures

1. Fix the hook's eye in the. Ensure that you secure the thread at the hackle before winding close turns of foundation thread about the fly's body to its tail.

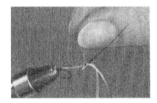

2. Tie three cock pheasant tail fibers to the fly body's extension to create the tail. Then, trim off the excesses.

3. Tie in a length of latex of natural color, after which you tie in a piece of bright yellow floss. When tying the floss, go in the anti-clockwise direction because the fly also tends towards that direction. The length of the latex should be enough for the winding to go on about ten times. After this winding, trim off the excesses and then go back to tie the thread at the hackle.

4. Wind and tie off the piece of yellow floss to get the fly's underbody.

5. Wound about ten turns of latex string for the body of the fly.

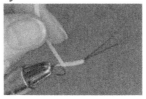

6. Tie off the latex string, and then trim the excesses close to the knot.

7. Before you go ahead to re-fix the hook, make a wrap knot at the point of the hackle to stop the latex string that you used to tie the body from loosening.

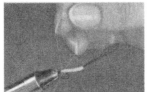

8. Re-position the hook so that its edge is in the vice. To make it easier to wind the hook on hackles, you should only fix its curve in the vice.

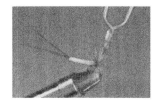

9. Tie in the two hackles, wind them off, and then tie them in place. Afterward, you can cut off the excesses.

10. Finish the fly with a wrap knot. If you find it difficult to tie a wrap knot with the flat hook's eye, then you can try the double half-hitch finish.

11. Remove the hook from the vice, and then use a black or brown-inked waterproof felt-tip pen to mark the body of the fly. Afterward, leave it to dry.

All-In-One Fly (Dry fly)

Tools and Materials

- A pair of google-eyed beads.

- Tail: A string of foundation thread.
- Wings: Hackle Fiber tails.
- Tying thread
- Loose Hackles
- Hooks

Procedures

1. Wound close turns of foundation thread to the tail's position.
2. Get a mass of hair tails and prepare them by tying them at a point from their ends. This step should be done in a way that the ends tend outwards in a broom style to form the tails. You are not to cut off the excess ends.
3. You can make the body of the fly and then finish by tying the thread at the wing position of the dry fly.
4. Tug at the hair strands evenly over the back of the body, just as it is illustrated below.

5. Tie the hair down at the portion for the dry fly's wings.

6. To make the wings, tug the remaining hair strands backward and then force them upwards by winding a series of clockwise turns of thread around the bottom. Finish this step by placing the thread behind the wing, exactly at the point where the hackle is.

7. The wing may occur as a single bunch or may be split into two bunches.

8. Tie in one of the cock's hackles and then wound the tying thread across the eye of the hook.

9. Wound the thread on the first hackle before proceeding to tie it off.

10. If you work with one more hackle, wind it through the first hackle and then tie it off.

11. Trim the excess hackles, and then finish off the fly.
12. If you like, you could trim the edges of the wings. The wings in the picture below were trimmed.

Optic Lure (Wet fly)

Tools and Materials

- Hook: 10

- Body Hackle: Cock Hackle

- Wings: Goat fur

- Body: Black or red thread strings.

- Eyes: Darkly hued beads with a black lacquer coating.

- Floss

Procedures

1. From the point where the lure is, leave enough room at the position of the head for a pair of eyes. Here, red and white color lure was used to make the project attractive.

2. The eyes shown here are a merged pair of darkly hued beads that were first lacquered black and then left to dry before they were eventually stained.

3. The eyes should not be too big relative to the lure.

4. Position the pair of beads (the ones meant for the eyes) right at the front of the wings and then tie them down on the hook's shank with the alternating diagonal turns technique.

5. To ensure that the eyes are fixed securely on the head, use the figure-eight turn technique to

wound them from the top. Thereafter, you can proceed to return the thread back to its normal winding line.

6. Finish the fly.

Stonefly Nymph

Tools and Materials

- Hook: 10
- Thread: Brown, yellow, or copper wire.
- Underbody: Strips of lead foil to form a hump on top of the hook.
- Hackles: Weighted shrimp fly
- Body Hackle: Buff cock hackle.
- Fly body Hackle: Weighted shrimp fly
- Body: Light green wool
- Back: Several coats of clear heavy lacquer, from the hook eye to the hook bend.

Procedures

1. Start by making the hook's shank by winding a yellow string of thread closely and firmly to the tail area. The hook used here is a 4-inches long-shank.

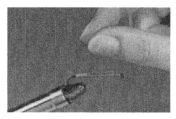

2. Cut out about two pieces of lead wire, each of body-length, while ensuring that each piece has the same thickness as that of the hook.

3. Tie in one piece of wire string on the shank's farther end so that the end of the wire is just centimeters away from the hook's eye. Afterward, bind the whole length of the wire string to the shank at a point close to the thread's turns.

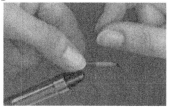

4. Bind the other length of lead wire across the end of the shank, and then work your way to the tail.

5. You could use a pair of needle-nose pliers to straighten the lead coils after you have bound them in.

6. Use an orange-colored and waterproof marker to color a few of the shortest, curved, and stiff fibers surrounding the bottom of a white swan primary feather.

7. Once the coloring dries up, pull off two fibers and then tie them off at the tail position so that one curves inwards and the other one curves outwards. You can color the piece again if need be.

8. Mark out a strip about 150mm long and 2mm wide on a latex sheet of natural color.

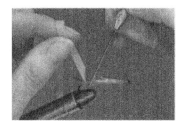

9. Cut out the latex strip while ensuring that you do not damage the ends.

10. Make one end of the strip narrow before tying in the tapered end of the strip above the hook's shank. Then, go ahead to wound the tying thread to the eye of the hook.

11. Use a dubbing needle to cover the shank with glue.

12. Ensure that the narrow end of the strip is very close to the hook's eye. Then, wind the strip towards the eye while ensuring that you keep the tension on the latex string low. Ensure that you make each turn with the overlapping technique.

13. Continue to wind the strip about until you cover half the length of the shank. This step finishes the segmented part of the nymph's body.
14. Wound the rest of the latex strip tightly to the eye, and then hold them down with the tying thread.
15. Trim off the ends of the surplus latex, and then take wide turns of thread down the body till you get to the segmented part.
16. Color the segmented part with an orange waterproof marker. Work the marker from right to left. Afterward, leave the color to dry.

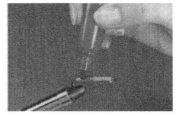

17. Draw a line with a brown waterproof marker along the segmented back of the nymph. This technique will be in similitude to the dark lines of the actual fly. This time, work the marker from left to right. Leave the color to dry.

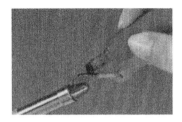

18. Create a loop of tying thread of about 75mm length at the end of the segmented section. Then, leave the loop hanging before winding the thread towards the eye.

19. Cut off a short length of rabbit fur that is dyed an orange color. Then, ensure that the long hair tufts are pushed closely together. From the bunch of furs, pull out as much underfur as possible.

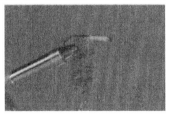

20. Open the loop and then fix the fur at the center. Fix a pair of hackle pliers to the end of the loop, and then leave it so that loop is displaced loosely.

21. Use both of your hands to spread the fur about until it is arranged evenly along the loop. Push the fur carefully until about 2/3 of the length of hair is piled at the loop's left side. Then, 1/3 of the length is pushed to the right.

22. If the fur was spread in such a way that it does not fill the whole length of the loop, gently move the hackle pliers upwards until its mouth just grips the bottom of the fur.

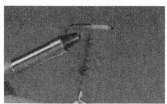

23. Twist the loop until the fur is properly twined about the string.

24. While holding the hackle pliers in one hand to ensure the loop is taut, immerse your other hand in the water to moisten the fur. As you do this technique, be careful not to pull the fur out of the loop.

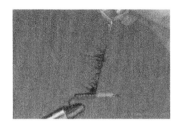

25. Wind on the fur and loop like a wet-fly hackle before pulling the fur carefully towards each of the tails.

26. Unwind the tying thread as far behind as needed before tying off one end of the loop.

27. Trim off the excesses of the fur that lies on top of the body so that the cases of the latex wings can lie flat.

28. To make the wing's cases, trim two pieces of natural-colored latex to the shapes shown below. Use a straight pair of scissors to cut out the sides

and the 'V' part and a curved pair of scissors to cut the shaped ends. Ensure that the width of the 'V' has the same width as the body.

29. Color the latex wing cases with an orange waterproof marker, and then leave them to dry.
30. Color the outer edges of the wing cases with a brown waterproof marker, and then leave it to dry.
31. Tie the first wing case into position using about two to three thread turns.
32. Use another string of tying thread of about 75mm to create another loop to tie the first wing case. Ensure that you leave the loop hanging and that you wound the thread to the eye.

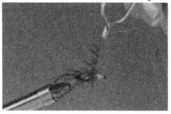

33. Prepare, spin, and wind on another branch of fur before tying it off with the tying thread.

34. Trim off the excess fur on top of the body just like you did before.

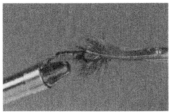

35. Tie on the second wing case before going ahead to trim off the surplus latex.

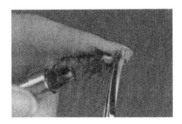

36. Pick out about two or more fibers (of a tinted orange color) from the swan feather to create the antenna. Then, tie the first antenna on top of the head. The antenna has to be shorter than the length of the tail fibers.

37. Tie the second antenna, and then cut off the excesses of both antennae.

38. With as many strings of thread as possible, make a neat wrap knot beneath the antennae. Ensure that you lacquer the knot only.

39. Use an orange-colored and water-proof marker to color the whole head. Then, you can leave it to dry.

40. Use a brown and water-proof marker to draw out a line along the top of the head to the hook's eye. Pass the tip of the marker through the antennae.

41. If needed, you can color any marks on the body again.

42. You are done!

Evolution Stonefly (Nymph Fly)

Tools and Materials

- Head: Brown, black, or gold.
- Hook: Curved nymph, stonefly hook, #6 for a large bead, #8 for medium, #10 for small.
- Thread: Brown, black, gold.
- Lead Wire: Standard
- Rib: Vinyl D-Rib, brown
- Antennae: Brown, black, tan.
- Tail: Brown, black, tan.
- Wing case: Turkey feather, brown, black, or tan.
- Abdomen: Dark hare's ear, black, gold.
- Thorax: Dark Hare's ear, black, gold.
- Legs: Barred rubber legs, brown, black.

Procedures

1. Fix the stonefly bead on the tip of the hook, and then place the hook at the tip of a vice. After doing that, push the bead head out of the way to a point far behind it. Next, tie the tying thread directly behind the hook's eye, and then wound the thread about it as many times as possible.

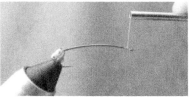

2. Choose two goose boots that will be used for the front antennae.

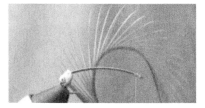

3. Tie in the goose biot antennae to the hook's eye. After that, proceed to knot the tie in before cutting off the excess ends of the rope.

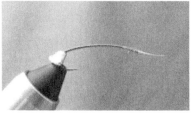

4. Push the stonefly bead head to the front of the hook. Then, place it above the tie-in point of the goose biot antennae.

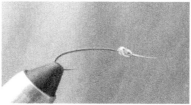

5. Wind the tying thread about the length of the hook's shank.

6. Then, tie two straight strings of lead-free wire on either side of the hook's shank to get the stonefly to have a flat and broad profile. Ensure that the length of each wire string that you use is about 2/3 of the length of the hook's shank. Pass the ends of the wire through the bead head on either side and then use the tying strings to keep them secure.

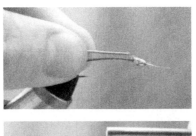

7. Wound the thread strings totally around the lead wire while ensuring that you push the thread windings to the back as you move.

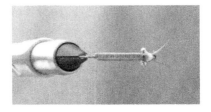

8. Tie in a length of the D-rib to start the ribbing process for the fly's abdomen. After doing that, the D-rib will be placed underneath the hook's shank. This technique will help ensure that the D-rib is out of the way as you tie the tail.

9. With a little dubbing, wind a dubbing ball around the point where you want the goose biot tails to be fixed.

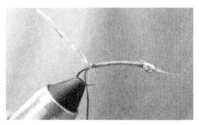

10. Choose two goose biots for the tail and then tie them in.

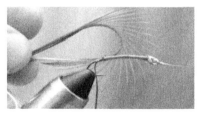

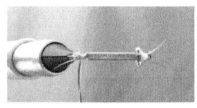

11. Make a rough abdomen that is about half the length of the hook.

12. Make the fly's ribs by winding the V-rib forward in a direction opposite the one you made the abdomen tend towards. Then, tie it off.

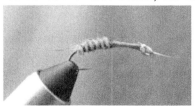

13. Make the fly's thorax by adding three wing cases and some legs made with rubber. Choose a length of dappled turkey feather, and then cut out a V-shaped hole on one end to mimic the shape of a stonefly wing case.

14. Tie in the first wing case the exact way it is shown here. Then, hold it down with either three or four wraps of thread. Ensure that you apply the right pressure on the wing case to slightly lift off the fly's body.

15. Wrap the dubbing about the thread's windings, and then use this technique to build the fly's thorax.

16. Cut off the excess ends of the turkey's feather.

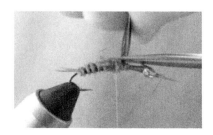

17. To get the second wing case, repeat the techniques utilized for the first wing case above. Tie in the wing case made from the turkey's feather, and then dub the thread wrappings over it.

18. Choose one strand of barred rubber legs.

19. Tie in one strand of the legs in front of the second wing case while ensuring that you stay at one side of the fly. Hold the legs in place by winding thread strings severally around it.

20. Repeat the technique above for the other side of the fly. Then, tie in a single strand of barred rubber legs to the front of the second wing case. Now, the fly should have a pair of back legs and a pair of front legs.

21. Tie in this last wing case the same way you did the first and the second.

22. Dub the thread wraps in a forward direction while ensuring that the thread is right in front of the rubber legs and right behind the bead head.

23. Finish with a whip knot before tying off your thread.

24. Add head cement to the thread wrappings before going ahead to cut off the excess lengths of dubbing fiber.

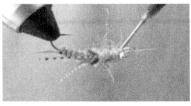

25. Trim the legs to equal lengths.
26. You are done!

Evolution Mayfly Clinger (Nymph Fly)

Tools and Materials

- Head: Nymph-head evolution, brown, olive, black, small, or medium-sized.
- Hook: Standard nymph hook 2XL, #12 for a large bead, #14 for medium, #16 for small.
- Thread: Tan, olive, or brown.
- Lead-free wire: Standard
- Rib: Ultra wire, gold.
- Tail: Pheasant tail, natural, olive, or brown.
- Abdomen: Hare's ear, brown, olive, or chocolate brown.
- Thorax: Hare's ear, brown, chocolate.

- Wing case: Pheasant tail, olive, or brown.

Procedures

1. Place the evolution bead head onto the mouth of a hook, and then align it towards the edge of the vice. Fix a tying thread directly to the back of the bead head.

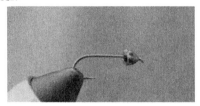

2. Tie in two strings of lead-free wire on either side of the shank's hook to get a flat and broad body. Each strip should be of a length that's half that of the hook's shank.

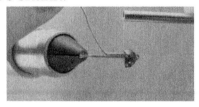

3. Pass the ends of the lead-free wire into the bead head, and then use your tying thread to wind them together. This technique will ensure that the fly comes out with a narrow shape.

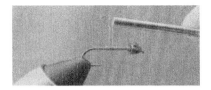

4. Tie in a piece of ultra-wire for the fly's ribs.

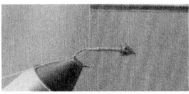

5. Pick out three pheasant fibers for the tail, and then tie them in.

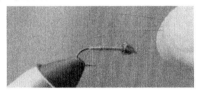

6. Use the tying thread to tie the figure-eight wrap. This technique will help pull strings apart. Then, to hold the fibers in position, apply beads of head cement.

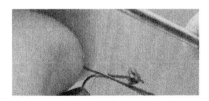

7. Dub the abdomen with the dubbing technique you will use for a hare's ear.

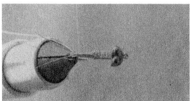

8. Wind the ultra-wire forward to make the ribbings for the abdomen. Then, use the pair of scissors to trim the abdomen to get something neat.

9. Pick out a mass of pheasant tail fibers that you can use to make the fly's wing case. Then, you can go ahead to tie them in.

10. To make the thorax, use more of the hare's ear dubbing. To get it to protrude out the more, you

could make the ties with a hairy thorax. For the legs, pull out spikes from the dubbings.

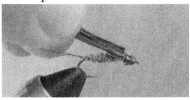

11. Pull the tail fibers forward and across the thorax to come out with a wing case.

12. Tie off the wing case behind the bead head by winding the thread around it severally.

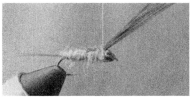

13. Cut off the excess pheasant tail.

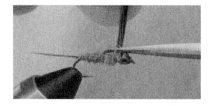

14. Finish with the whip knot before tying off the thread. Then, add drops of head cement.

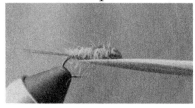

15. Trim the top of the fly as well as the bottom to come out with a thin side profile for the fly.

16. You are done!

Chili Pepper

Tools and Materials

- Hook: Size #14 to #2 streamer hook.
- Bead: Nymph head metal tungsten bead.
- Weight: Lead Wire.
- Thread: Fire Orange
- Tail: Burnt orange marabou.
- Tail Flash: Copper Flashabou.
- Hackle: Brown, ginger.
- Body: Copper tinsel chenille.
- Collar: Fire orange thread.

Procedures

1. Fix the bead to the hook and then place the hook in the vice with the hook heading towards the direction of the bead's small hole.

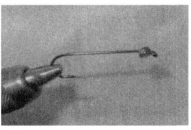

2. Wind enough wire turns about the hook's shank till it covers about 2/3 of its length.

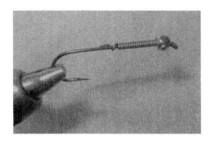

3. You will see an unused part of the wire. That part is there for the thread string to be wound upon so that it doesn't roll off.

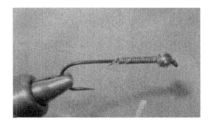

4. Once the wire string is wrapped with thread, wrap the thread back to the barb and then back to the wire string. This technique forms the marabou tie-in section.

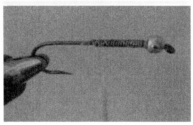

5. Get a Marabou plume, and then cut off a bit of marabou from the stem.

6. To make a smooth move, tie in the marabou at a point just behind the wire string.

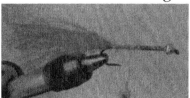

7. Get a little portion of the tail and then tie it on top of the first marabou. You can get even shorter tails so that you wouldn't get too short strikes. You could use long tails, though; it doesn't really matter much here.

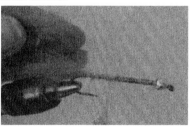

8. Cut the corners of the flash packaging, as this technique makes it much easy for you to tug at each strand one by one.

9. To get four strands of flash, fold two strands of flash around the thread string.

140

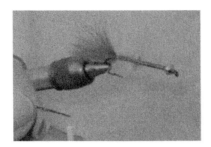

10. As you slide the flash up the thread string, you will get the chance to fix the thread wherever you want it to be. And here, the thread should be displaced at the tail's far end.

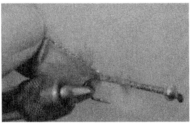

11. Repeat the procedure above for the side of the threading that is closer to you.

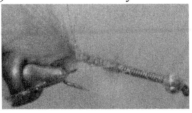

12. Once you get the flash tied in, pass the thread string back to the end of the wire.

141

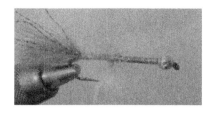

13. The Conranch chili pepper saddle has all the colors of the chili pepper. You could also use hackles that occur in the brown ginger color and the red furnace color.

14. Tie in the hackle by the tip and then ensure that the dull side faces you. This technique allows you the grace of making twists on each wrap of thread. This way, the dull side of the hackle faces the side opposite you.

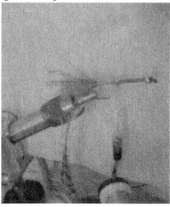

15. Tie in the chenille behind the wire string.

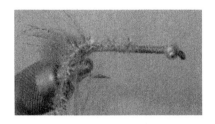

16. Make the hackle stand straight up so that you can begin the winding technique in a reverse direction. Ensure that the dull side of the hackle faces away from you as you wind the thread string through. The hackle is usually wrapped around the body so that it's flat down. You should also check to see that you cut off the barbs as you get to make the last wrap. For a clean finish, you should make the final wrap with a bare stem.

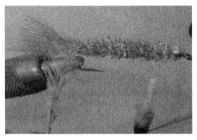

17. Finish the wraps off with an orange-colored collar.

18. Add dots of red to the collar with a tube of Tulip fabric paint.

19. To make a pupil for the fly's eye, add a spot of black.

20. Then, leave the black spot to dry up before finishing the eye with any finish of your choice. This will help your project stand the test of time.

Swimming Nymph

Tools and Materials

- Hook: Swimming nymph hook, #12.
- Thread: Uni 8/0 wine.
- Head: Nymph head.
- Body: Tackle with hackle beaver dubbing, mahogany.
- Shellback: Virtual nymph Flexi-body, dark tan.
- Thorax: Tackle with Hackle Beaver dubbing, mahogany.
- Tail: Peacock eye fibers, naturally dyed red.
- Gills: Peacock herl, naturally dyed red.
- Dorsal stripe: White, embroidery floss.
- Legs: Dyed march brown.
- Ribbing: Small, copper-brown.

Procedures

1. Fix the bead to the hook, and then tie in about three peacock eye fibers. This technique will make for a tail at the hook's bend. Tie in the first tail above the shank for the middle tail. Lastly,

you can use a dubbing ball to divide the two sides of the tails.

2. Tie in the embroidery floss to make the stripes dorsal and above the hook. For the underside of the hook, use ultra-wire. Then, for the gills, use peacock herl.

3. You can go ahead to dub the abdomen to any length of your choice.

4. Fold the peacock herl over and then tie them in on either side of the body. That technique will form the gills. Afterward, you could fold the embroidery floss above the body and then tie it in to make the dorsal stripes. Make the abdomen's ribbings with ultra-wire, and then tie them in. It is only when you get to this stage that you should cut off the peacock herl. Lastly, fold the dorsal stripe back towards the hook's curves.

5. Tie in the wing case that has been precut into 3mm for a size 12 hook. This tie-in should be above the curve. Then, tie-in a Brahma hen hackle for the cups of the legs. This tie-in should be above the curve.

6. Dub the thorax to a size of your choice. Fold the legs across the fly, and then tie it behind the bead. Next, pull the wing case across the fly's head before going ahead to tie it behind the bead again. Lastly, finish the fly with a whip knot.

Whirling Dervish

Tools and Materials

- Hook: Any wet fly hook, #12-#16.
- Thread: Mono, Clear.

148

- Bead: Silver
- Tail: any long and mottled fiber.
- Body: Gold.
- Underwing: Gray
- Overwing: Red
- Collar: Natural rabbit fur.

Procedures

1. Fix the bead to the hook and add a CDL (Coq de Leon) tail.

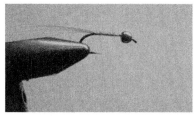

2. Add a gold body braid.

3. Add a few fibers of gray foxtail and ensure that the tail fibers do not pass the tail's outermost end.

4. Place some red fox above the gray fox tail fibers to build up the wing. Again, ensure that you do not pass the tails.

5. Make a dubbing loop, and then add a bit of a string of natural rabbits to the circle. To the front of the wing, add twisted dubbing loops. Add these loops to the back of the bead too. Then, go ahead to stroke the fibers back towards the direction of the tail as you wind the dubbing loop. Then, finish the fly with wrap knots.

6. Then, use cement glue to hold the wraps down.

7. You are done!

Black Ghost Streamer

Tools and Materials

- Hook: A long streamer hook.
- UNI waxed thread, #8, Black.
- Hare line Saddle Hackle, yellow.
- UNI flat embossed French tinsel, silver.

151

- Hare line Antron Yarn, Black.
- Whiting American Streamer Hackle, White.
- Hare line Jungle Cock.

Procedures

1. Get your tying thread and then, wind it about the curved part of the hook before tying it in. Pick out several fibers of saddle hackle, and then align the edges. Afterward, tie them in at the hook's curve. Once you have tied in your tail, pass the thread back through the posterior part of the hook.

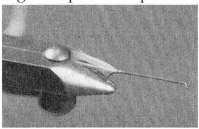

2. Tie behind the hook's eye the French Tinsel, then hold it in place by winding the thread string around it. Once you are done winding the end to the point of the fly's tail, pass the thread string back to the tie you made in front of the Tinsel.

3. Tie in the Antron Hare line behind the hook's eye, and then wind the thread backward, towards the tail region. Secure the hare line to the hook's

shank by passing your thread string behind the hook's eyes again. This technique will help the fly's body come out a little bulky, in a way that its body tapers towards the ends. Afterward, tie off the yarn and then cut off the excess strings.

4. Wind the tinsel across the yarn's body to get the fly ribbed. You can follow through with this technique by working with your hands or using a rotary vice to get the fly ribbed. Tie off the tinsel behind the hook's eye, and then trim off the excesses.

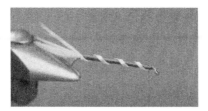

5. Select another mass of yellow hackle and then tie it beneath the hook's shank. The Hackle should

have roughly the same density as the fly's tail. Turn your vice around and then, tie the hackle in beneath the hook's shank.

6. Tie in the wing's feathers. Then, pick out two American Hackle feathers and have them measured so that they only extend the tail's length by a bit. Cut off the excess fibers and then tie in one feather at each side of the hook's shank. Hold down the feathers loosely, trim the ends, and then use a string or thread to make the fly's head.

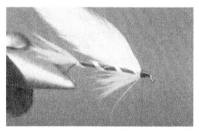

7. To make the streamer's eyes, tie in the cock on either side of the hook's shank. Then, trim the

butts with windings of thread. After that, finish with a whip knot.

8. Add any finish of your choice to the fly's head so that it can stand the test of time.

9. You are done!

Berg's Caddis Larvae

Tools and Materials

- Hook: #10
- Bead: Mayfly Brown tungsten bead
- Thread: 3/0 white

- Body: Large and round rubber legs
- Body coatings: Clear, flexible coating

Procedures

1. Fix a 1/8-inch mayfly nymph-head bead on a #10 scud hook before mounting it on a vice.

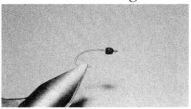

2. Start to wind the tying thread a few inches behind the bead. Ensure that you incorporate the wire string several times before stabilizing the bead by pushing the wire through it.

3. Tie in a few inches of natural rubber legs just behind the bead. This rubber will be the material of the body.

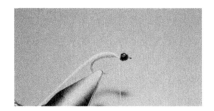

4. After stretching the material past a few inches, wrap it tightly down the hook's curve. Do that before you pass the thread string behind the bead to make an underbody with a regular surface.

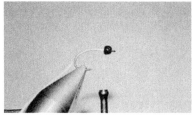

5. Start to wind the material about the book as you stretch the body material. Then, release the tension of the material bit by bit as you continue to wrap it around the hook. This technique will help to keep the outline of the body tapered.

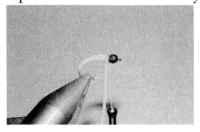

6. Tie the material off just behind the head before cutting it off. Then, finish with a wrap knot before cutting off the excesses.

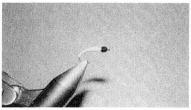

7. Coat the surface of the fly's body with clear and flexible coatings.

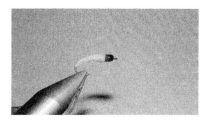

8. For the fly to come out more real, you can touch the first few shoulder sections with brown acrylic paint.

9. You are done!

Voodoo Stonefly

Tools and Materials

- Hook: #2 – #12
- Bead: Mayfly Brown or Stonefly Black.
- Thread: Black or dark brown.
- Underbody: Vernille, brown, tied along the hook's shank.
- Dubbed body: Squirrel dubbing, ¼ black, ¼ dark brown, ½ brown.
- Ribs: Gold wire, stripped peacock herl.
- Wing case: Dark mottled turkey tails.
- Thorax: Squirrel dubbing, ¼ black, ¼ dark brown, ½ brown.
- Hackle: Mottled hen hackle, brown.
- Gils: White or cream ostrich herl.
- Tails and antennae: Hackle quill stems, dark brown.
- Weight: Hackle quill stems, dark brown.
- Weight: Lead Wire.

Procedures

1. Fix the bead to the hook, and then fix the hook to your vice. Afterward, begin to wind your tying thread just behind the hook's eye.

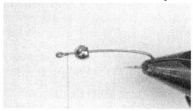

2. Tie on two hackle stems for the antennae and then finish with a whip knot. Afterward, start threading behind the bead.

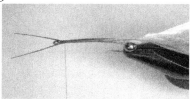

3. Wrap the thread strings along the hook's shank just above the hook's barbs. Afterward, pass the thread back through the hook's mid-shank. Then, tie the first string of vernille on one side of the

shank. Wound the thread string to a part before the beads start, then trim the excesses. Repeat this technique on the hook's other side.

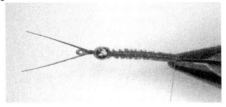

4. With your thread string at the hook's curve, place a little dubbing material there, and then tie in your gold ribbings. After that, tie in the peacock herl at the end of the hook.

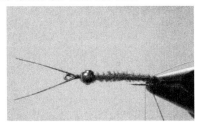

5. Tie in the hackle stem tails one by one on either side of the body. While doing that, ensure that you use a ball of dubbing material to separate the tails. Once that is over, cover the body with thin layers of head cement. Leave the adhesive to dry.

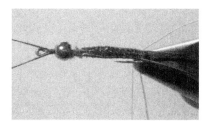

6. Dub the whole body from the tail to the bead head before winding the thread back to the middle of the hook's shank.

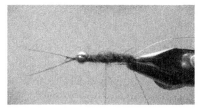

7. Wind your peacock's quills to the middle of the hook's shank. Then, leave large spaces between each winding so that the dubbing material shows. Then, wrap a strip of golden wire about the quill in the opposite direction.

8. Tie in the length of oak turkey by the edges, and then tie in the hen hackle feather with the tips.

162

While you follow up with this technique, ensure that the tips lie beneath the thorax before you finally tie in the ostrich herl.

9. Dub the thorax and then wind the ostrich's herl to a point close to the head while ensuring to leave space between each winding. Then, thread the hen hackle around the ostrich before pulling the wing case over. Tie in the wing case, and then dub the collar. You can finish the fly by tying a whip knot. The part of the bead that bears the eyes should be painted red.

10. You are done!

Little Black Stone

Tools and Materials

- Hook: #14—#18
- Thread: Black
- Head: Silver nymph-head, with the eyes, painted a red color
- Abdomen: Pheasant tail fibers dyed a black color.
- Thorax: Peacock herl dyed black.
- Tail: Pheasant tail fibers dyed black.
- Rib: Silver wire, small-sized.
- Wing case: Stonefly style, folded back.

Procedures

1. Wind the tying string to wind the hook's shank from half of its length to the bead. Then, fix the silver wire to it. After this procedure, use the tying thread to the point where the hook begins to curve. Use a whip knot to hold the tie in place.

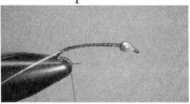

2. Fix two Pheasant tail fibers to the hook's shank, with the tips pointing outwards for the tails. Afterward, pass the thread to the front about 2/3 inches back up from the hook's shank.

3. Roll the ends of the fiber's tail into a twisted rope before winding the yarns towards the point the tying thread stopped in the above process. Then, tie down the fibers.

4. Wind the wire string in a reverse direction about the tail fibers while ensuring that you hold down the place where you fixed the threads.

5. Fix the Flashabou wing case to the body before winding the thread string back to the head.

6. Fix three peacock herls to the body of the fly.

7. Wind the tying string forward to the back of the bead. Ensure that you hold down the bead with thread windings.

8. Turn the wing case forward before making three threads turnings over the Flashabou. Afterward, pull back the rest of the material.

9. Fold the Flashabou forward when you get to the middle of the wing case. Then, finish the fly with a whip knot.

10. Apply cement glue to the thread and then color the eyes a deep red color to finish.

11. You are done!

The end… almost!

Hey! We've made it to the final chapter of this book, and I hope you've enjoyed it so far.

If you have not done so yet, I would be incredibly thankful if you could take just a minute to leave a quick review on Amazon

Reviews are not easy to come by, and as an independent author with a little marketing budget, I rely on you, my readers, to leave a short review on Amazon.

Even if it is just a sentence or two!

So if you really enjoyed this book, please...

>> Click here to leave a brief review on Amazon.

I truly appreciate your effort to leave your review, as it truly makes a huge difference.

Chapter 7

Fly Tying Frequently Asked Questions (FAQ)

1. What are the things needed to start out with the tying of flies?

You will need all the tools mentioned in this book — bobbin, whip finishers, vices, hackle pliers, and all others.

2. How can I choose the right size of fishing hook?

Hooks are measured using a 'Size' and 'Aught' scale. The middle of the plate bears the figure—1/0, while the farther end bears the figure—10/0. A hook of size 6 is a lot smaller than a size 6/0 hook. The baitholder hook is what you need to bear worms and insects. It has two barbs on its shank that prevent the bait from falling off the mouth of the hook. An octopus hook is best for catching leeches and minnows. So, you can work with a #6 or #4 for minnows. The Aberdeen hook is used for insects, so for that, you can go for the #4 size.

3. **How do I know the right size of thread to use for fly tying?**

The more zeroes you see for the dimension of a thread string, the thinner it is. The common thread sizes include the 8/0 for dry flies, the 6/0 for nymphs, the 3/0 for large flies, and so on.

4. **Is there any disadvantage of getting my tying thread string waxed?**

The issue with this technique is that the wax can clog up bobbins and also increase the thread's weight.

5. **What is a bonded thread?**

A bonded thread is a round piece that is made by bonding parallel filaments together. They are resistant to scratches than the majority of the flat thread strings and will fetch you wonderfully segmented bodies for flies.

Conclusion

Now that we have gotten to the end of this book, you'd notice that the art of tying flies is quite simple as long as you get yourself acquainted with the preliminary techniques and the other essential tips. When you start out, ensure that you have all the tools and materials within your reach. Then, proceed to try out the projects outlined in this book. They are all beginner-friendly and will guide you through every step of the way. If you end up with a fly that doesn't look too much like the final image provided in this book, you can try again until you get what you want. You should also be safety-conscious as you will be working with a lot of tools with sharp edges.

I wish you lots of fun tying flies and I'd love to know that you were able to catch all the fishes you have always wanted.

Happy fly tying!